CODE: STEM

SMART HOMES

Real-world coding projects made fun

Max Wainewright

WAYLAND
www.waylandbooks.co.uk

First published in Great Britain in 2019
by Wayland

Credits:
Editor: Elise Short
Designer: Matt Lilly
Cover Design: Peter Scoulding
Illustrations: John Haslam

Every attempt has been made to clear copyright.
Should there be any inadvertent omission please
apply to the publisher for rectification.

ISBN: 978 1 5263 0875 7

Printed and bound in China

Picture credits:
Shutterstock: NicoElNino 6, VCoscaron 12,
petrmalinak 14, Andrey_Popov 18, Sean Pavone 24,
Photographicss 28, Dreamstime: GarcÃa Juan 26.

Wayland
An imprint of
Hachette Children's Group
Part of Hodder and Stoughton
Carmelite House
50 Victoria Embankment
London EC4Y 0DZ

An Hachette UK Company
www.hachette.co.uk
www.hachettechildrens.co.uk

We recommend that children are supervised at all times when using the internet.
Some of the projects in this series use a computer webcam or microphone. Please
make sure children are made aware that they should only allow a computer to access
the webcam or microphone on specific websites that a trusted adult has told them to
use. We do not recommend children use websites or microphones on any other
websites other than those mentioned in this book.

The website addresses (URLs) included in this book were valid at the time of going to press. However, it is possible that contents or
addresses may have changed since the publication of this book. No responsibility for any such changes can be accepted by either the author
or the Publisher.

Scratch is developed by the Lifelong Kindergarten Group at the MIT Media Lab. See http://scratch.mit.edu
Images and illustrations from Scratch included in this book have been developed by the Lifelong Kindergarten Group at the MIT Media Lab
(see http://scratch.mit.edu) and made available under the Creative Commons Attribution-ShareAlike 2.0 licence (https://creativecommons.org/
licenses/by-sa/2.0/deed.en). The third party trademarks used in this book are the property of their respective owners, including the Scratch
name and logo. The owners of these trademarks have not endorsed, authorised or sponsored this book.

Contents

Introduction

In this book you will learn how computer technology is used in modern homes and buildings. You'll find out about how this technology is changing the way we live, making our lives easier and our homes more secure.

We'll spend some time looking at how some devices use smart technology. Alongside that we will have a look inside the computer code that connects up the components and brings devices to life.

You'll use the algorithms and ideas that are used to control devices within buildings to create your own coding programs. These programs will help you to understand how things work – and set you on the road to dreaming up your own ideas for the house of the future!

There are lots of different ways to create code. We will be using a website called Scratch to do our coding.

Type **scratch.mit.edu** into your web browser, then click Create to start a new project.

Let's start by looking at the important parts of the screen in Scratch:

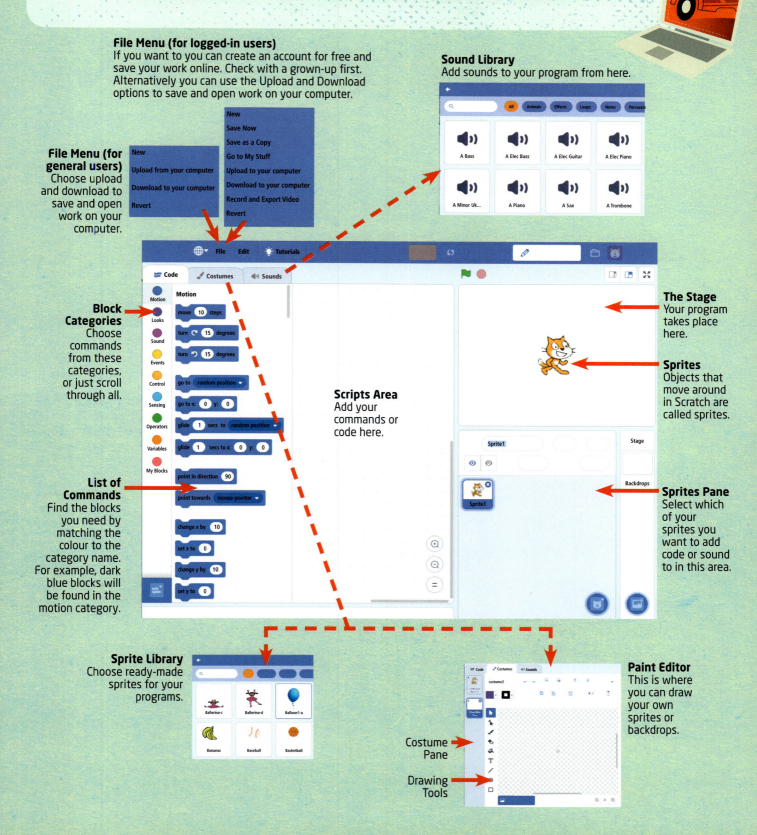

File Menu (for logged-in users)
If you want to you can create an account for free and save your work online. Check with a grown-up first. Alternatively you can use the Upload and Download options to save and open work on your computer.

Sound Library
Add sounds to your program from here.

File Menu (for general users)
Choose upload and download to save and open work on your computer.

Block Categories
Choose commands from these categories, or just scroll through all.

List of Commands
Find the blocks you need by matching the colour to the category name. For example, dark blue blocks will be found in the motion category.

Scripts Area
Add your commands or code here.

The Stage
Your program takes place here.

Sprites
Objects that move around in Scratch are called sprites.

Sprites Pane
Select which of your sprites you want to add code or sound to in this area.

Sprite Library
Choose ready-made sprites for your programs.

Paint Editor
This is where you can draw your own sprites or backdrops.

Costume Pane

Drawing Tools

Smart Homes

Technology has always played a big role in the home and other buildings. Over 2,000 years ago, the ancient Romans invented simple underfloor heating. Candles gave way to gas-powered and then electric lights. New inventions continue to improve today's buildings.

But now computers are taking an ever-increasing role in how different parts of a building work. Let's build our own house with code to see how this works. The house will have a number of automatic lights (and music!) that switch on and off as the Scratch Cat walks around.

STEP 1 - The Stage

We need to draw the background first, so click **Stage** in the **Sprites pane**.

STEP 2 - The Backdrop

Click the **Backdrops** tab.

For help go to:
www.maxw.com

6

STEP 3 - The sky

Click **Convert to Bitmap**.

Choose light blue.

Select the **Fill** tool.

Click in the Drawing Area to draw the sky.

Click the Undo tool if you make a mistake.

STEP 4 - The ground

Choose dark green.

Select the **Rectangle** tool.

Set the rectangle to **Filled**.

Drag the mouse to draw the ground.

STEP 5 - Draw the house

We need to draw things inside the house, so just draw a simple silhouette of the house in white.

Choose white.

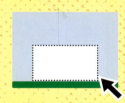

Use the mouse to draw a large rectangle for the main part of the house.

Pick the **Line** tool.

Make the line thicker.

Draw three lines to give the house a simple roof.

Choose the **Fill** tool.

Click inside the roof to fill it in with white. (If the colour leaks outside the house, click **Undo** and look for any gaps between your lines. Join them up.)

STEP 6 · Get coding

We need the cat to be outside the house when the program starts.

Sprite 1

Click on the cat in the **Sprites pane**, to make sure that you assign the code to the cat, not the house.

Click the **Code** tab.

Now drag in this code:

```
when 🚩 clicked
go to x: -210  y: -115
go to front layer
set size to 50%
```

← Run this code when the green flag is clicked:

← Set the x and y co-ordinates to move the cat to the left of the screen (see page 30).

← Bring it in front of any other sprites.

← Shrink the cat down to half its normal size.

🚩 **Click the green flag to test this part of the code.**

STEP 7 · Move it

Now drag in these four separate sections of code to make the cat move.

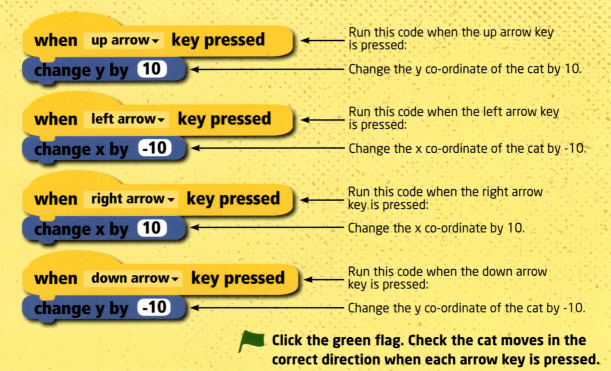

```
when up arrow key pressed
change y by 10
```

← Run this code when the up arrow key is pressed:

← Change the y co-ordinate of the cat by 10.

```
when left arrow key pressed
change x by -10
```

← Run this code when the left arrow key is pressed:

← Change the x co-ordinate of the cat by -10.

```
when right arrow key pressed
change x by 10
```

← Run this code when the right arrow key is pressed:

← Change the x co-ordinate by 10.

```
when down arrow key pressed
change y by -10
```

← Run this code when the down arrow key is pressed:

← Change the y co-ordinate of the cat by -10.

🚩 **Click the green flag. Check the cat moves in the correct direction when each arrow key is pressed.**

STEP 8 - Make a room

Let's draw the first room. To keep things simple, just draw a rectangle. In order to switch the light in the room off and on depending on whether the cat is in the room, we need the rectangle to be a sprite.

Hover over the **Choose a Sprite** button.

Click the **Brush** icon.

Click **Convert to Bitmap**.

Select the **Rectangle** tool.

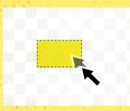

Drag out a yellow rectangle. (Yellow will stand for the room being lit up.)

Now drag your new room sprite inside the house.

 If the room is too big or too small, click the **Arrow** tool in the Drawing Area.

Then click on a corner and drag to adjust the size of the sprite, so it is almost a quarter of the size of the house.

We need to make the light in each room switch on when the cat walks into it. But before we code our house, let's take a moment to find out how a real smart house uses sensors to do this.

How it works

There are many different types of sensor that can be used to detect motion. We'll start by looking at a passive infrared motion detector or PIR.

As a human being (or animal) passes through the area of detection the PIR notices a slight change in temperature. It detects this change because a tiny amount of infrared radiation is emitted by the passer-by. The Fresnel lens focuses the radiation on to the PIR.

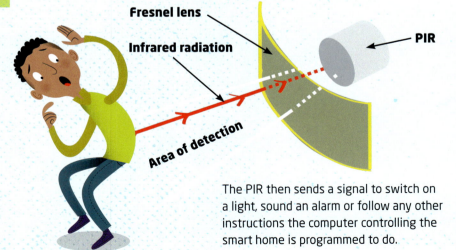

The PIR then sends a signal to switch on a light, sound an alarm or follow any other instructions the computer controlling the smart home is programmed to do.

STEP 9 - Sensor code

 Click the **Code** tab. Drag in this code for the room sprite to detect when the cat enters the room.

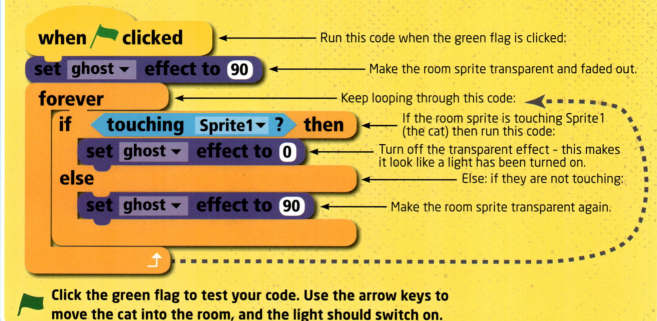

when ⚑ clicked ← Run this code when the green flag is clicked:

set ghost ▾ **effect to** 90 ← Make the room sprite transparent and faded out.

forever ← Keep looping through this code:

if touching Sprite1 ▾ **? then** ← If the room sprite is touching Sprite1 (the cat) then run this code:

set ghost ▾ **effect to** 0 ← Turn off the transparent effect - this makes it look like a light has been turned on.

else ← Else: if they are not touching:

set ghost ▾ **effect to** 90 ← Make the room sprite transparent again.

⚑ **Click the green flag to test your code. Use the arrow keys to move the cat into the room, and the light should switch on.**

STEP 10 - More rooms

We can create more rooms by duplicating the first one. This will copy all of the code too.

In the **Sprites pane**, right-click the room, then click **duplicate**.

Drag the new room into a space in the house.

Duplicate two more rooms, and position them like this in your house.

⚑ **Click the green flag to test your code. Use the arrow keys to move the cat around the house. Each light should switch on and off automatically!**

How about making music play automatically when the cat goes into a room? That would be cool!

STEP 11 - Automatic music

Click one of the room sprites in the **Sprites pane**.

Click the **Sounds** tab.

Click the **Choose a Sound** icon.

Select **'Dance Around'** or another sound clip.

STEP 12 - Code it

Click the **Code** tab.

play sound dance around ▼ until done

Insert this code block into the sensor code to make the room sprite play the music.

Test it!

Investigate

What happens if you try different numbers in the 'set ghost effect' code block?

What do the different effects do?

Code challenge

Try adding more rooms. Could you put one in the attic space at the top?

Add some furniture to the room sprites.

Listen to the other sound effects available . Can you find one that would be good in the bathroom. Maybe you could make the bath start running when the cat goes in the room?

Imagine it's a really hot day. How about having a fan that comes on automatically when you walk near it? You'll need to draw a new sprite to be the fan. Make sure you draw it in the middle of the Drawing Area. Your code will be similar to the room sprites' code, but instead of changing the ghost effect you will need to make the fan rotate - but only if the cat is near it.

Entry Phone and Camera

The first doorbells were invented nearly 200 years ago. The technology has developed considerably since then, and it's now quite common to find entry phones with cameras outside blocks of flats or in houses. With the use of mobile technology it's now possible to see who's knocking at your door even if you are on holiday.

As Artificial Intelligence (AI) develops, your house may soon be able to let you in automatically if it recognises your face! Let's create a doorbell.

STEP 1 - Remove the cat

Right-click on the cat sprite and click **delete**.

STEP 2 - Add a sprite

Click the **Choose a Sprite** icon.

STEP 3 - The button

Scroll through to find **Button1**. Click on it.

STEP 4 - Add the Music Extension

We need to add some extra code blocks to let us control the sound of the doorbell. This group of code blocks is called an extension.

Click the **Add Extension** button.

Click **Music**.

STEP 5 - Get coding

Drag this code into the **Scripts Area**:

when this sprite clicked
♪ **set instrument to (16) Vibraphone ▾**
♪ **play note 63 for 0.5 beats**
♪ **play note 59 for 1 beats**

Run this code when the button sprite is clicked:

Choose (16) Vibraphone.

Play note 63 for half a beat.

Play note 59 for a beat.

🚩 **Click the green flag to test this part of the code.**

If your computer has a webcam we can add a camera to the door bell to see who is calling! Remember to only use your webcam with websites you trust and people you know!

STEP 6 - Add the Video Extension

Add some extra code blocks to use the webcam.

Video Sensing

Click **Add Extension**.

Click **Video Sensing**.

STEP 7 - The camera

Modify your code to include the video camera:

when this sprite clicked
turn video on ▾
♪ **set instrument to (16) Vibraphone ▾**
♪ **play note 63 for 0.5 beats**
♪ **play note 59 for 1 beats**
wait 5 seconds
turn video off ▾

Turn the camera on when the button sprite is clicked.

Wait a moment.

Turn the camera off.

when 🚩 clicked
turn video off ▾

Add this second piece of code to make sure the camera is off when the program starts up.

 **Allow**

If you want your computer to use the camera then you need to click the **Allow** button the first time the program runs.

Code Challenge

Try to make your doorbell play a different tune.

♪ **play note 64 for 0.5 beats**

E (64)

Can you add a second tune? Either add another button with this tune, or work out a way of switching between them.

For help go to: www.maxw.com

Voice Control 1

Some modern buildings use voice control technology. Instead of pressing a button to switch on a light or turn up the heating, all you need to do is say 'turn lights on'. Let's look at how this works and build our own simple version using code.

You need a microphone for your computer to be able to do this project. There may be one built into it.

First, let's take a 'look' at the sounds around us by creating a program that can draw a simple waveform of the sounds detected by the computer.

Make sure it is selected and turned up by checking the settings program on your computer.

STEP 1 - How loud?
We need a variable that can store how loud different sounds are.

Click the **Code** tab.

Click the **Variables** category.

Click **Make a Variable.**

Type **level**.

Click **OK**.

To let Scratch use your microphone you need to click the 'Allow' button the first time the program runs.

Beware of other websites asking to use your microphone – check with an adult first.

STEP 2 - Add the Pen Extension

Add some extra code blocks to use the pen and drawing blocks.

 Click the **Add Extension** button.

 Click **Pen**.

STEP 3 - The code

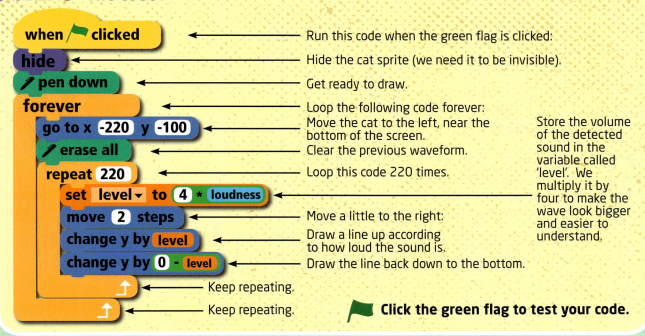

Run this code when the green flag is clicked:

Hide the cat sprite (we need it to be invisible).

Get ready to draw.

Loop the following code forever:

Move the cat to the left, near the bottom of the screen.

Clear the previous waveform.

Loop this code 220 times.

Store the volume of the detected sound in the variable called 'level'. We multiply it by four to make the wave look bigger and easier to understand.

Move a little to the right:

Draw a line up according to how loud the sound is.

Draw the line back down to the bottom.

Keep repeating.

Keep repeating.

🏴 **Click the green flag to test your code.**

Use calculations in your code by dragging operator blocks within other blocks. Make sure they snap into place correctly.

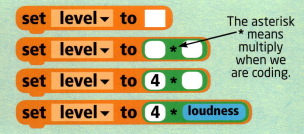

The asterisk * means multiply when we are coding.

How it works

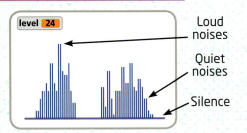

When you run your code a blue line will start moving across the screen. Speak into your computer's microphone and you should see a waveform appear. Try speaking at different levels, whispering and shouting! The louder your voice the taller the waveform will be. Try saying different words like 'switch on' and 'switch off' to see the 'shape' of the sound levels.

If no blue lines appear, or they are very small, check your microphone's settings.

Voice Control 2

Now we know how to detect the sound levels sensed by the computer, let's make a simple program that switches the lights on or off. The lights will change when our program 'hears' a command.

STEP 1 - Remove the cat

We're going to draw our house so we won't need the cat. Right-click on it and click **delete**.

STEP 2 - Add a sprite

Hover over the **Choose a Sprite** button.

Click the **Brush** icon.

Click the Undo tool if you make a mistake.

STEP 3 - The sky

Click **Convert to Bitmap**.

Choose dark blue.

Select the **Fill** tool.

Click in the Drawing Area to draw the sky.

STEP 4 - The ground

Pick dark green.

Select the **Rectangle** tool.

Set the rectangle to **Filled**.

Drag the mouse to draw the ground.

STEP 5 - The house

Draw a simple house shape in brown.

See step 5 on page 7 for help.

STEP 6 - Windows and a door

Choose the **Rectangle** tool.

Draw a blue door and four yellow windows (with the lights on).

STEP 7 - Duplicate costume

We need a second picture of the house with the lights out. Scratch calls this a second 'costume'. To make this we will duplicate the first one, then change it.

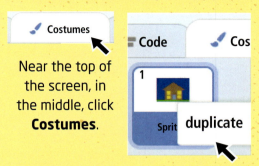

Near the top of the screen, in the middle, click **Costumes**.

Right-click the house icon **costume1** then click **duplicate**.

STEP 8 - Lights out!

Select the **Fill** tool and choose black.

Fill the windows in with black (so the lights are switched off).

The house should now have two costumes.

STEP 9 - The code

Click the **Code** tab, then add this code to make the lights switch on or off.

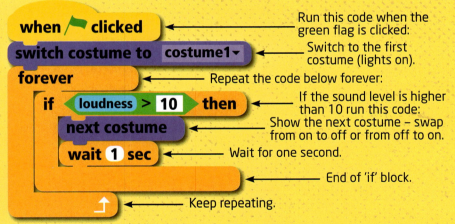

Run this code when the green flag is clicked:

Switch to the first costume (lights on).

Repeat the code below forever:

If the sound level is higher than 10 run this code:

Show the next costume – swap from on to off or from off to on.

Wait for one second.

End of 'if' block.

Keep repeating.

Click the flag to test your code. Try saying 'off' or 'on' to your computer ... or clapping. If your microphone is very sensitive the lights may flash off and on. If this happens try changing the value to 10, 20 or 30.

How it works

Our program doesn't really know what has been said. It just listens out for a sound then switches the lights on or off. Creating a more sophisticated program that really understands commands is a lot more complex. To do that we would need to analyse the shape of the waveform the computer records and compare it to a waveform that says 'on', 'off' or other words.

Home Robots

Have you already got a robot in your home? Over the next few years you may find more and more making their way into your house, cleaning your floors and windows, delivering your shopping, or even paintaing your walls!

But can robots really do these kinds of tasks properly? Let's have a look at how the code inside them works by making a robot vacuum cleaner.

STEP 1 - Remove the cat

Right-click on the cat sprite and click **delete**.

Our screen robot won't be able to vacuum up real dirt. But it will show us how a robot vacuum cleaner works out how to move around.

STEP 2 - Add a sprite

Hover over the **Choose a Sprite** button.

Click the **Brush** icon.

Now draw your robot cleaner. Make sure you show it in plan view – drawn from above. It needs to face to the right.

STEP 3 - Shapes and colour

Click **Convert to Bitmap**.

Choose a silver colour for your robot.

Select the **Circle** tool.

Choose the **Filled** option.

STEP 4 - Draw the robot

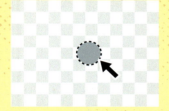

In the middle of the Drawing Area, draw a medium-sized circle – about one fifth of the Drawing Area.

Draw two yellow ovals to start creating the eyes.

Add black ovals to complete them.

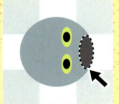

Draw a dark grey oval to start drawing the mouth.

Select the silver colour you used to start the robot.

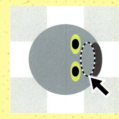

Draw over the dark oval to create a smile.

Add some lights, arms and any other details you want.

19

STEP 5 - Add the Pen Extension

Click the **Code** tab, then add some extra code blocks to use the pen and drawing blocks.

 Click the **Add Extension** button.

 Click **Pen**.

STEP 6 - Robot code

Add this code to make the robot move around. See page 23 for help on how to choose colours.

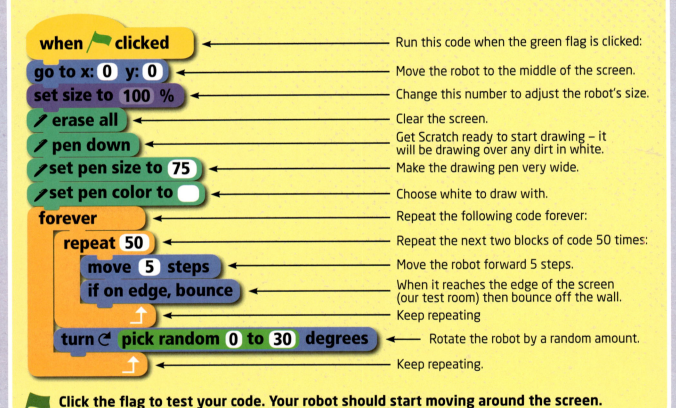

when 🚩 clicked	Run this code when the green flag is clicked:
go to x: 0 y: 0	Move the robot to the middle of the screen.
set size to 100 %	Change this number to adjust the robot's size.
erase all	Clear the screen.
pen down	Get Scratch ready to start drawing – it will be drawing over any dirt in white.
set pen size to 75	Make the drawing pen very wide.
set pen color to ⬜	Choose white to draw with.
forever	Repeat the following code forever:
repeat 50	Repeat the next two blocks of code 50 times:
move 5 steps	Move the robot forward 5 steps.
if on edge, bounce	When it reaches the edge of the screen (our test room) then bounce off the wall.
⬆	Keep repeating
turn ↻ pick random 0 to 30 degrees	Rotate the robot by a random amount.
⬆	Keep repeating.

🚩 **Click the flag to test your code. Your robot should start moving around the screen.**

To test our robot we need some dirt on the screen for it to sweep up.

Let's draw some small dots on the screen that the robot can draw over in white.

STEP 7 - Muddy shoes

 Add some muddy shoes by clicking the **Choose a Sprite** button.

 Click **Shoes2**.

STEP 8 - Add the mud

 Click the **Code** tab, then add this code to make the dirt appear when you click on the screen.

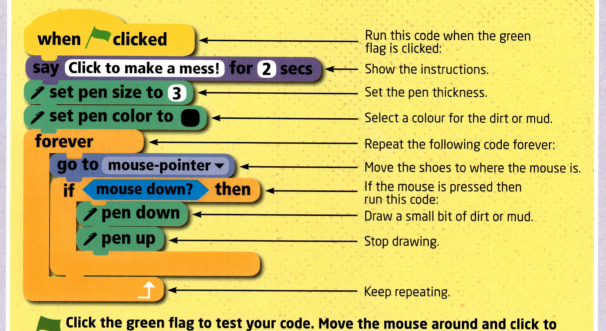

when 🏳 clicked	Run this code when the green flag is clicked:
say **Click to make a mess!** for **2** secs	Show the instructions.
set pen size to **3**	Set the pen thickness.
set pen color to ⬤	Select a colour for the dirt or mud.
forever	Repeat the following code forever:
go to **mouse-pointer** ▾	Move the shoes to where the mouse is.
if **mouse down?** then	If the mouse is pressed then run this code:
pen down	Draw a small bit of dirt or mud.
pen up	Stop drawing.
↰	Keep repeating.

🚩 **Click the green flag to test your code. Move the mouse around and click to make a mess! See how long it takes the robot to vacuum everything up.**

Our robot works, but it doesn't use any intelligence. It just moves around randomly.

If only there was a way we could make the robot detect where the dirt is, it would work much more effectively!

STEP 9 - Upgrade the robot

We need to add a 'sensor beam' that will look for any dirt or mud.

Sprite1   Shoes2

In the **Sprites pane** click on **Sprite1** - your robot.

 Costumes

Click the **Costumes** tab.

STEP 10 · Add a sensor

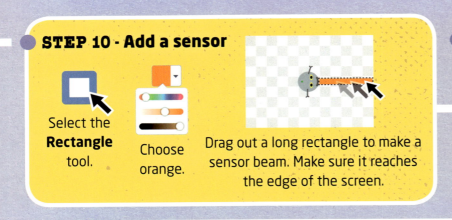

Select the **Rectangle** tool.

Choose orange.

Drag out a long rectangle to make a sensor beam. Make sure it reaches the edge of the screen.

STEP 11 · Add the Music Extension

Click the **Code** tab.

Click **Add Extension**.

Click **Music**.

STEP 12 - Upgrade the code

Change your code as below.

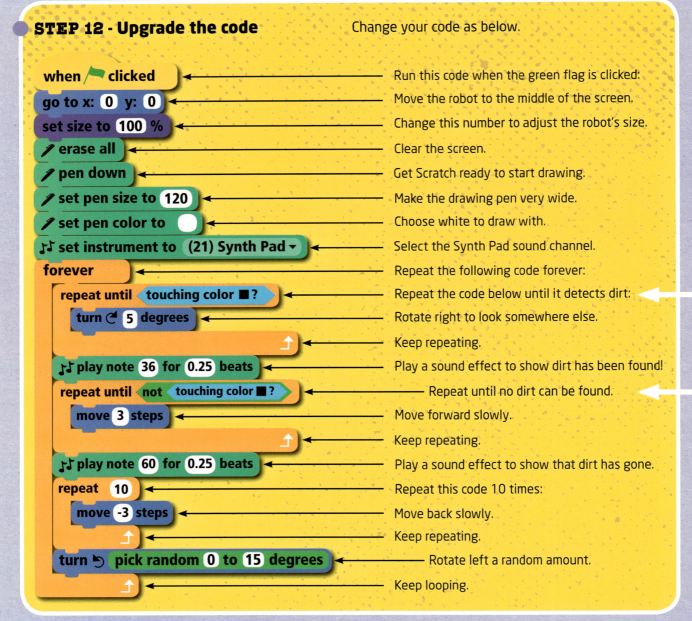

when 🏳 clicked — Run this code when the green flag is clicked:

go to x: 0 y: 0 — Move the robot to the middle of the screen.

set size to 100 % — Change this number to adjust the robot's size.

erase all — Clear the screen.

pen down — Get Scratch ready to start drawing.

set pen size to 120 — Make the drawing pen very wide.

set pen color to ⬜ — Choose white to draw with.

♫ set instrument to (21) Synth Pad ▾ — Select the Synth Pad sound channel.

forever — Repeat the following code forever:

  repeat until touching color ■? — Repeat the code below until it detects dirt:

    turn ↻ 5 degrees — Rotate right to look somewhere else.

  ↰ — Keep repeating.

  ♫ play note 36 for 0.25 beats — Play a sound effect to show dirt has been found!

  repeat until not touching color ■? — Repeat until no dirt can be found.

    move 3 steps — Move forward slowly.

  ↰ — Keep repeating.

  ♫ play note 60 for 0.25 beats — Play a sound effect to show that dirt has gone.

  repeat 10 — Repeat this code 10 times:

    move -3 steps — Move back slowly.

  ↰ — Keep repeating.

  turn ↺ pick random 0 to 15 degrees — Rotate left a random amount.

↰ — Keep looping.

Set the colour by clicking inside the square. Next click on the pipette and then click on a colour somewhere on the Stage.

touching color ⬛ ?

Create this part of the code by dropping a 'not' block inside the 'repeat until' block. Next drop in a 'touching colour?' block.

touching color ⬛ ?

not

Investigate

What happens if you change the pen size in the robot's code from 120 to a smaller number? Increase the amount the robot turns when it's looking for dirt. Does it still find it as well? If you drop dirt in the corner of the screen can the robot still find it?

Code Challenge

Make your robot bigger. Does that help?

Try to adapt your code so the robot finds dirt quicker.

Create a workforce of mini robots:
- start by shrinking the robot, by changing the set size code.
- change the colour of its eyes, so they are not the same colour as the dirt. Another robot may think they are dirt and try and vacuum them up!
- use a 'go to random postition' code block at the start to prevent all the robots starting at the same place.
- now duplicate your mini robot a few times!

Burglar Alarm

There are many ways in which technology can be used to keep us safe.

Modern buildings include smoke detectors to detect fires. Security systems can be built to check if windows or doors are opened, or to sense anyone moving around. In this project we will make a simple alarm that will detect if anything is nearby.

STEP 1 - Get moving

Drag in these separate sections of code to make the cat move.

Run this code when the left arrow key is pressed:

Run this code when the right arrow key is pressed:

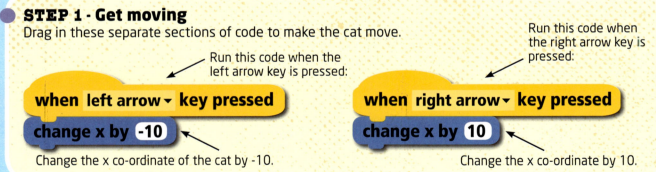

```
when  left arrow ▾  key pressed
change x by -10
```

```
when  right arrow ▾  key pressed
change x by 10
```

Change the x co-ordinate of the cat by -10.

Change the x co-ordinate by 10.

STEP 2 - Select the backdrop

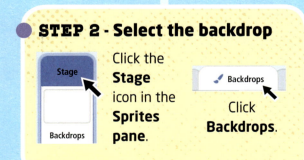

Click the **Stage** icon in the **Sprites pane**.

Click **Backdrops**.

STEP 3 - Draw the sky

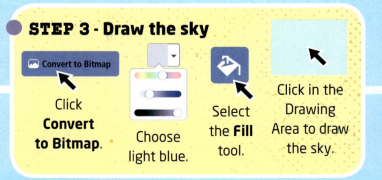

Click **Convert to Bitmap**.

Choose light blue.

Select the **Fill** tool.

Click in the Drawing Area to draw the sky.

STEP 4 - Draw the ground

Select the **Rectangle** tool, then choose green.

Set the rectangle to **Filled**.

Drag the mouse to draw the ground.

STEP 5 - The house

Draw a simple house.

See step 5 on page 7 for help.

Click the Undo tool if you make a mistake.

You can add more detail to your house when your code is finished.

STEP 6 - Add the alarm

Add an **alarm sprite** by clicking the **Choose a Sprite** icon.

Button1

Click **Button1**.

Drag the alarm on to the house.

STEP 7 - Add the Music Extension

Click **Add Extension**.

Click **Music**.

STEP 8 - The code

Add the code below to make a siren sound when a noise is detected.

when 🏳 clicked — Run this code when the green flag is clicked:

forever — Loop the following code forever:

if distance to sprite1 < 160 then — If the cat is near the alarm, then run this code:

♪ play note 60 for 0.5 beats — Play a sound as the alarm.

↺ — Keep looping.

🏳 **Click the flag to test your code.**

Investigate

What happens if you change the distance in the green block to a number larger than 160? How about smaller numbers?

Where is the best place to put the alarm?

Burglar Alarm - Audio

Let's make a real burglar alarm using Scratch!

In this project we will make a real alarm that will listen out for anyone coming near your computer! First we need some code that can detect sound. If a sound is detected, we can make our code trigger an alarm. Your computer needs to have a built-in microphone, or you will need to plug one into it. If it has a webcam, it will probably work for sound too.

STEP 1 - Basic code

Drag in the code below to make a basic alarm.

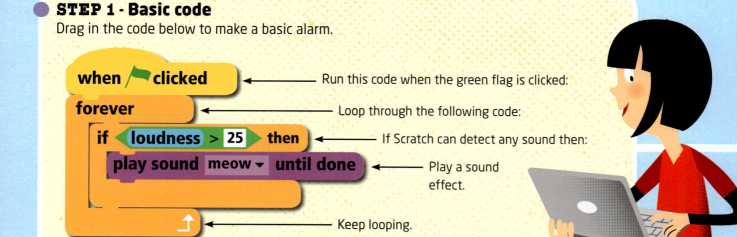

when 🏳 clicked — Run this code when the green flag is clicked:

forever — Loop through the following code:

if loudness > 25 then — If Scratch can detect any sound then:

play sound meow ▾ until done — Play a sound effect.

↰ — Keep looping.

STEP 2 - Test it

🏳 **Click the green flag to test your code.**

Try making a noise and see if the cat starts to meow!

If nothing happens try checking the microphone is plugged in, then check your settings (see page 14). You may need to try a different value than 25 depending on your computer and microphone.

STEP 3 - Add the Music Extension

Click **Add Extension.**

Click **Music.**

STEP 4 - Alarm upgrade

Our code can detect sounds, but a cat meowing isn't going to scare off many burglars! Change your code to create a siren effect. Start by making a **variable** to store the pitch of the siren.

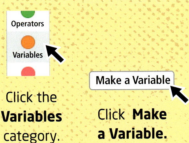

Click the **Variables** category.

Click **Make a Variable.**

Type **pitch.**

Click **OK.**

STEP 5 - The siren

Change your code to include a siren by varying the pitch.

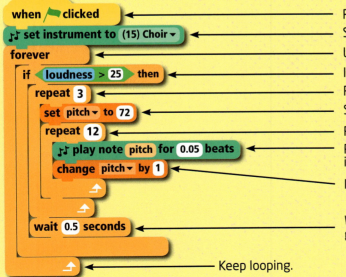

Run this code when the green flag is clicked:
Select (15) Choir.
Loop the following code forever:
If the computer can detect a noise:
Repeat this code 3 times:
Start the pitch at 72.
Repeat this code 12 times:
Play a note for a very short time. (Try 0.1 or 0.2 if your computer doesn't play it clearly.)
Increase the pitch.

Wait half a second (or the alarm may 'hear' itself going off - and keep on forever!).

Keep looping.

 Click the flag to test your code.

Burglar Alarm - Video

The previous alarm project used a microphone to detect sounds. Most burglar alarms use sensors and cameras to check for intruders.

In this next project we'll find out how we can use the computer's webcam to detect movement and trigger an alarm sound.

STEP 1 - Make a variable

We need a **variable** again to store the pitch of the alarm sound.

Click the **Variables** category.

Click **Make a Variable.**

Type **pitch**.

New variable

New variable name:

pitch

◉ For all sprites   ◯ For this sprite only

More Options

Cancel   OK

Click **OK**.

To let Scratch use your webcam you need to click the 'Allow' button the first time the program runs.

Beware of other websites asking to use your webcam. Always ask an adult you trust first.

✓ **Allow**

STEP 2 - Add the Music Extension

Click **Add Extension**.

Music

Click **Music**.

STEP 4 - The code

Change your code to include a siren by varying the pitch.

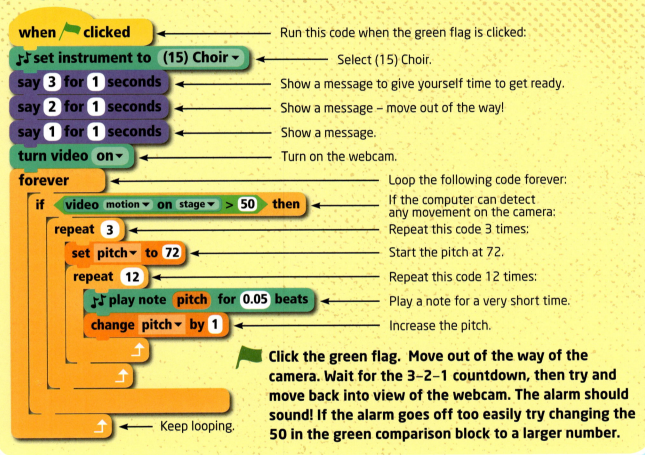

when ⚑ clicked ← Run this code when the green flag is clicked:

♪ set instrument to (15) Choir ▼ ← Select (15) Choir.

say 3 for 1 seconds ← Show a message to give yourself time to get ready.

say 2 for 1 seconds ← Show a message – move out of the way!

say 1 for 1 seconds ← Show a message.

turn video on ▼ ← Turn on the webcam.

forever ← Loop the following code forever:

if video motion ▼ on stage ▼ > 50 then ← If the computer can detect any movement on the camera:

repeat 3 ← Repeat this code 3 times:

set pitch ▼ to 72 ← Start the pitch at 72.

repeat 12 ← Repeat this code 12 times:

♪ play note pitch for 0.05 beats ← Play a note for a very short time.

change pitch ▼ by 1 ← Increase the pitch.

↻ Keep looping.

⚑ **Click the green flag. Move out of the way of the camera. Wait for the 3-2-1 countdown, then try and move back into view of the webcam. The alarm should sound! If the alarm goes off too easily try changing the 50 in the green comparison block to a larger number.**

How it works

The webcam takes pictures and turns them into information that the computer can store. It does this by storing the picture as millions of tiny squares, called pixels. The colour of each pixel is stored as a number.

The video motion code block takes one photo, then another a fraction of a second later. It then compares the colour stored for each pixel and checks to see how much it has changed. It then counts up the changes and uses the total to say how much motion it can detect.

Bugs and Debugging

When you find your code isn't working as expected, stop and look through each command you have put in. Think about what you want it to do, and what it is really telling the computer to do. If you are entering one of the programs in this book, check you have not missed a line. Some things to check:

Join block properly:

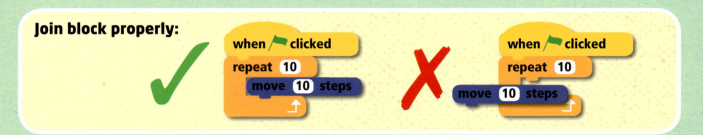

Select sprites before adding code:

Before you add code to a sprite, click on it in the Sprites pane. This will select it and make sure the code is assigned to it.

X or Y?

y Don't mix
↑ them up!
→ x

The right size

The wrong size sprite may stop your code working. Use the grey grid squares to judge how big your sprites should be. Use the Arrow tool to adjust the size or use the 'set size %' code block.

Right colour, wrong code?

Be precise. Many code blocks look very similar but do completely different things!

Position variables and values carefully

Don't type in variable names.

Don't just drop them on top of blocks.

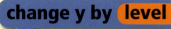

Drag them until a glowing white circle appears.

The value block will then snap into place.

Tips to reduce bugs:

• When things are working properly, spend time looking through your code so you understand each line.
Experiment and change your code, try out different values.
To be good at debugging you need to understand what each code block does and how your code works.

• Practise debugging! Make a very short program and get a friend to change just one block while you aren't looking. Can you fix it?

• If you are making your own program, spend time drawing a diagram and planning it before you start.

• Try changing values if things don't work, and don't be afraid to start again − you will learn from it.

Glossary

AI (artificial intelligence) – software that does more than just follow steps. AI systems respond with apparent intelligence to outside events.

Algorithm – rules or steps followed to make something work or complete a task.

Bug – an error in a program that stops it working properly.

Code block – a draggable instruction icon used in Scratch.

Debug – removing bugs (or errors) from a program.

Degrees – the units used to measure angles.

Hardware – the wires, chips, sensors and physical parts of a system or computer.

Icon – a small clickable image on a computer.

Loop – repeating one or more commands a number of times.

Pitch – the degree of highness or lowness of a sound.

Pixel – a tiny square on a computer screen, combined in their thousands to display pictures.

Random – a number that can't be predicted.

Right click – clicking the right mouse button on a sprite or icon.

Sensor – a device that measures something in the real world, such as how far away an object is, and sends the answer to a computer as a number.

Sequence – commands that are run one after another in order.

Software – a computer program containing instructions written in code.

Sprite – an object with a picture on it that moves around the stage.

Stage – the place in Scratch that sprites move around on.

Steps – small movements made by sprites.

System – a combination of software, hardware, sensors and information.

Transparent – if something is transparent, you can see through it very clearly

Variable – part of a program that stores a value that can change, for example the score in a game.

Waveform – a diagram showing a sound as a wave shape where loud parts are higher, and quiet parts are lower.

Index

FURTHER INFORMATION

Gifford, Clive. *Get Ahead in Computing* series. Wayland, London, UK: 2017.

Wood, Kevin. *Project Code* series. Franklin Watts, London, UK: 2017

Wainewright, Max. *Generation Code: I'm an Advanced Scratch Coder.* Wayland, London, UK: 2017.

CODE: STEM

Series contents lists

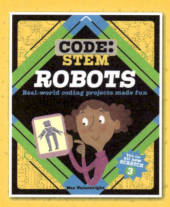

Introduction • Project:Following Instructions • Project: Sensors • Project: Sensing the Way • Project: Taking Orders • Project: The Robot Arm • Project: Robot Arm Game • Project: Walking and Talking • Bugs and Debugging • Glossary • Index

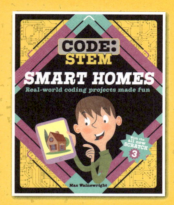

Introduction • Project: Smart Homes • Project: Entry Phone and Camera • Project: Voice Control 1 and 2 • Project: Home Robots • Project: Burglar Alarm • Bugs and Debugging • Glossary • Index

Introduction • Project: Blast Off! • Project: In Control • Project: Gravity • Project: Jetpack • Project: Jetpack Game • Project: Satellites • Project: Return to Earth • Bugs and Debugging • Glossary • Index

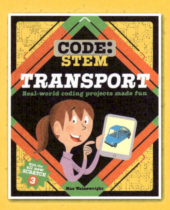

Introduction • Project: Automotive Technology • Project: Drones • Project: Destination Drone • Project: Self-Driving Cars • Project: Hoverboard Scooters • Project: Hoverboard Game • Bugs and Debugging • Glossary • Index

WAYLAND
www.waylandbooks.co.uk